MY HEART IN EXILE

Kush Ha Mim

Author's Tranquility Press
Marietta, Georgia

Copyright © 2022 by Kush Ha Mim.

All rights reserved. No part of this publication may be reproduced, distributed or transmitted in any form or by any means, including photocopying, recording, or other electronic or mechanical methods, without the prior written permission of the publisher, except in the case of brief quotations embodied in critical reviews and certain other noncommercial uses permitted by copyright law. For permission requests, write to the publisher, addressed "Attention: Permissions Coordinator," at the address below.

Kush Ha Mim/Author's Tranquility Press
2706 Station Club Drive SW
Marietta, GA 30060
www.authorstranquilitypress.com

Ordering Information:
Quantity sales. Special discounts are available on quantity purchases by corporations, associations, and others. For details, contact the "Special Sales Department" at the address above.

My Heart in Exile/Kush Ha Mim
Hardback: 978-1-957208-32-9
Paperback: 978-1-957208-33-6
eBook: 978-1-957208-34-3

Table of Contents

Inside looking out 3
A Moment too Long 5
Cry 6
Here we are 7
Here without you 8
In the grey 9
Incomplete 10
Love-Oh love! 11
A Moment too Long 12
Nostalgia 13
Since you've been away 14
Someone else does 15
Stranded 16
Such is life 17
Teeming Up 18
The jury is out 19
The melee I'm in 20
Through it all 21
Way back when 22
When I was where I was 23
Heartfelt 24
I'm just saying 25
The shape of my heart 26
Exiled Outside Looking In 27

Peace and blessings, I dedicate this book to my beautiful umm (mother). May the MOST HIGH reward her peace and *blessings*

ACKNOWLEDGEMENTS

Peace and blessings my acknowledgments go out to the MOST HIGH for blessing me with a remedy to cope with all that I have to cope with, and may he forgive me and have mercy on my soul, and may he bless all who has my wellbeing as their interest and wish to see me in peace I greatly appreciate you all peace and blessings

Inside looking out

From my vantage point, this is my point of view
It's lonely at the top I'm exiled away
But I view love on the horizon out of the blue
And as the moonbeams down, I'm in disarray
 Inside looking out no shadow concealing doubt
I balance the scale judging my heart
Out and about in around and throughout
I can honestly say that I'm doing my part
Outside the darkest days are joyful compared
For nothing compares to being exiled, I confess
I'm running love's gauntlet, but I'm unimpaired
Though filled, I'm empty love has a void to congest
Helpless, I help myself to a dose of second-guessing
Has love deserted so? That's one I'd like to know
My poor wounded heart needs caressing
Chances I've taken backfired, but there's a die I'd like to throw
Your distant love, I sit and watch from the distance
A distant memory I am, but what a sight to behold
In this unknown land, how did I found the entrance?
Exiled away from love and what remains to be told

Kush Ha Mim

A Moment too Long

You've been away a moment too long
A long lost love I've been longing for
That moment of my life is a barren land
A drought too long I need love
That long moment keeps expanding
I wasn't prepared for such an ultimatum
It's a new feeling, one I'm unaccustomed to
For its been a moment too long
The sun has risen and set too many times
Without us enjoying the sight on the horizon together as one
And the evening star has been stunning
Followed by the beautiful moonlit skies
But I haven't taken full notice because you've been gone a moment too long
It's been too long a moment to pretend and cast aside as if it's nothing
It's just a moment too long even to remember how long it's been
Since the very moment, we departed

Kush Ha Mim

Cry

I have the right to, and I might do
But as I write to you, it's a plight to
Cry!
I won't just spite you all day and night
You give me a fight you soar high as a kite you
Cry!
Emotions you incite
You're Wrong, and your right you
Grasp me so tight you set me in flight you
Cry!
You want to see that sight, you know just that I might
You Test the strength of my might
You so heavy, so light you
Cry!
Would it somehow excite you?
Or would my pain fright you
Your memory so slight you forget I delight you
Cry!
Who cares? I just might
You don't, but it's alright you don't think of me at night you do it out of spite you
Cry!
I just might ...

Kush Ha Mim

Here we are

As I peer through the dark window of my mind
Your bright eyes haunt me. I should have been over you by now
But apparently, I'm to be antagonized
I love you, and you love me, but here we are
Where going nowhere up nor down
I love to hear your voice though it hurts
For someone else arms your wrapped in at night
This is where we are awaiting our fate
Circumstances hold us back from instant decision
I swear I hear your heartbeat! Or is that mine?
Oh well, it all seems the same we used to be one ...
Now here we are. I'm attached you're separated
I carry the weight of our love, didn't you know?
I feel helpless in exile-what more can I say?
Watching you drift slowly away-here we are

Kush Ha Mim

Here without you

The gloom does it again; it always makes me recollect
It has no means to offend though what's buried it resurrects
I'm here without you that's true it's been so long I forgot
And I'm to be amongst the few that it love won't I rot
Days fly by I watch them; I swear wind carries your laughter!
Rays shine down I catch them; my life is a beautiful disaster
And I'm abandoned in such state I wish you well nonetheless
My heart and soul you grate No love behind me none abreast
But for those who'll never leave, they're constantly ready
My burden they help to heave they're rampantly steady
Still, I long to see you but even still, I'm moving on
I've dreamt plenty up to be you, but I refuse to be loves pawn

Kush Ha Mim

In the grey

Paralysis has taken over, immobilizing my heartache
Severing love's tendons back to the grey, I relapse
Grey skies grey enthusiasm grey matter of being
I ponder why I stress so much about you, and I've yet to reach a conclusive state of reason
Perfectly sane though love plays deceptively with my psyche
My tries of extirpating your memories fail miserably
And back to the grey, I relapse
In the grey skies, the sun peaks shortly then disappear behind grey clouds teeming with tears
I've heard of a fabled place where southward bound it never rains
This must be the paradise where love and my lover resides
While in the grey looming gloom, I sit and watch grey clouds
My zest for you waned in time as love ran amok
And in the grey existence of love's aftermath, I search for a pulse
Shortly thereafter, in the grey, I relapse

Kush Ha Mim

Incomplete

My better half, you're the best part of me
The reason is I'm incomplete
You're the missing pieces to my life's puzzle
The finishing touch to my life's masterpiece
So with you not present, I'm incomplete
You're the missing cornerstone to my life's temple
A precious piece of my completion
The missing link to my life's chain of events
Without you, I'm incomplete
I'm out of sync with harmony without you
Unable to be in tune with love
And also off-beat with the tune of my heart
For without your guidance, I'm incomplete
You're the final pieces to the bridge of my life
Connecting both sides as one
Keeping a fair balance with events of my life
So with you missing, I'm affected greatly
For without you, I'm not the same I'm incomplete

Kush Ha Mim

Love-Oh love!

Rarely depressed am I ever but am I not human?
Being emotionally stable is roughly separated from loves
Union
As I gradually grow, your love fades away as dusk fades to night
But that could be a misconception love do tend to spite I dream
of you, but the memories we shared seems like a dream
That leaves my reality disarranged was it all just a scheme?
In exile, such thoughts cross my mind, don't you care?
Or you're just too occupied with no love to spare?
I think of you wondering if you do the same often
Mesmerized by those eyes, I'm so easily lost in, but there's little
sign little faith you love me less than those I hate
Though two wrongs still leads us left, love goes on straight
Rarely regress do I ever, but your love I remember so well
With little distractions to distract memory becomes a spell
I'm holding on to a wisp of hope, but can I really let go?
You keep me in constant upheaval I wanted you to know

Kush Ha Mim

A Moment too Long

Memories of a beautiful summer haunt my present state
A reminder of how bland summers are now at the present rate
White sand between my toes love's boat my heart and soul rows
In the moonlight, the waves grow I sail with you in tow Memories of a beautiful fall haunt my sentience
Reminders how bland falls are now such a pestilence
Auburn leaves falls on our picnic as we laugh in love as fools as the leaves falls, so does our heart's as our love glimmer like jewels
Memories of a beautiful winter haunt my fiefdom
A reminder of how bland winters are now when shall relief come?
Love's coat keeps us warm, oblivious to the snow-filled freeze
By love's fireplace, we lay in love naked as the wind-blown trees
Memories of a beautiful spring haunt my tenor
A reminder of how bland springs are now affecting my temper
Love's roses scented with a sweet aroma fill the air with love
Love birds on the edge of love to us take flight with love's shove

Kush Ha Mim

Nostalgia

Once upon a time still feels like yesterday
When during that time, nothing takes your memory away
There's no love like yours, none worthy to contend
I'm forced to dwell on your memories, refusing to pretend
It all depends on my mood though I conjure memories a lot
My mind is a continuous saga, and you're the plot
I long for the times when our future looked bright
Now my present was the future, but some things were not right
This was not what we dreamt; how did this come to past?
How I ended up being exiled from a love so vast?
Now my days I spend longing and my nights far too long
How beauteous be the day when I'm back where I belong
Life is so unpredictable my predicament attest
Though reminiscing ill make it another night at best
How much longer must I suffer?
Does no one hear my cry?
My love has been ignored though I long for a reply

Kush Ha Mim

Since you've been away

My heartbeat drowns out the sound
As my mind thinks out loud
Loneliness has been my companion
Ever since you've been away
I ponder if you think of me or not
Do I trot across your memory?
Do you stare at the moon and reminisce?
Such thoughts I ponder since you've been away
I'm usually asleep by this time of night
But my conscience has been heavy lately
I am getting restless, and it's frustrating
This is how it's been since you've been away
I rarely get the chance to speak my mind
Just to tell you what I've been meaning to say
Forgive me if I sound a little too brash
But that's just how it's been since you've been away

Kush Ha Mim

Someone else does

Since I cannot:
Make love to you
Hold you and caress you
Be there to protect you
Impregnate you
someone else does
The list goes on But my pen refuse
I must not spell it out, for I'll bring on
Agony, so I'll pause ...
Alright, now I am back, I've cleared my mind
I cannot accept losing you
But as I was saying, Since I longer Skip your heartbeat
Bring shimmer to your soul Keep you infatuated
Take your breath away
someone else does
Yes, I am jealous
No need to deny the fact
Out of mind once out of sight
Once that sight catch wind ... Of someone else

Kush Ha Mim

Stranded

On first thought second the third go-around
I've spent a fortune on love now it's cheap by the pound
And to think you fooled me so-A a standing ovation!
Crown you, the queen of hearts-Outstanding coronation!
As I reminisce, you're a splinter wedged in my memory bank
To sabotage my wellbeing, need I be more frank?
Sigh ... But still, I love you it's not my choice to decide
Half mine, half yours, it's fitting you get the choice to divide!
Darkness falls, and a cold chill stifles the evening air
An exclamation point to my mood both exceedingly austere
Yet so overwhelming bereaving me of peace-Love the widow
Haunting as it doesn't love out dates the willow?
Confused as I am, you take little pity though I needn't none
In love we stalemate I'm stranded but along you run
But life goes on I say it often; it's obvious enough
In my neutralized state, I still travel a road so rough

Kush Ha Mim

Such is life

I see you finally get the drift
I had to smile at the thought
Life goes by so fast and swift
So vile this life I sought
But then again, such is life
Only God knows our destiny
I wish to have you as my wife
You bring out the best in me
I won't be gone forever
There's a decision you need to make
It's not quite now or never
But there's a position you need to take
No rush, so take your precious time
But it's over here or there
Close your eyes you'll hear love's Mime
He speaks, I swear

Kush Ha Mim

Teeming Up

Drip, drop, drip, drop!
Rain lands on my cheeks to help me cry
And soon it will stop The love I long for will pass me by
I grasp at it ...
But it flees and smiles at me
I'm harassed by it
I know it long's for a child by me
Here comes the sun
Now you'll never know I cried
I must be the pun?
I'll set all jokes aside
With no pun intentionally intended
Love will understand
With our love intentionally upended
Tears mount up in my glands

Kush Ha Mim

The jury is out

While I was wandering, I was wondering
Just pondering my abandoning
I found it quite astonishing
My heart still beats no oxygen
I'm seeking refuge from the jinn
Love love's me not it plays to win
To swim in love, I need a fin
If I died in love, who's next to kin?
My heartache aches I need an inn
Pinned down in love who pinned the pin?
I fight, I fight I can't give in
Alright, alright, I might begin
I blow out smoke right threw a grin
I'm lost in love; how I got in?
Love's roundabout I spin and spin
The jury is out my sentence is in

Kush Ha Mim

The melee I'm in

Love is in the air, so I may die ... asphyxia!
Such a dreaded despair caused my dyslexia
I'm to read between the lines but what a terrible feat
And I'm to work love's mines in this terrible heat
Blinded by love's moonlight
Surrounded by the dark
And I just soon might find it to be a lark
Still, love is in the air, so I might as well
Love comes in pairs, but I just can't tell
Though stated on the charts
I still choose a blade in a well filled with hearts
I withdrew a spade!

Kush Ha Mim

Through it all

Through it all, I'll smile to mask my dishevelment from view
Through it all, I'm going strong though agony lingers on cue
I'm in love with too many my heart seems to brew
Through it all, I'm going strong though my mind is in a hue
How did life come to this? What was it that I missed?
Through it all, I'm going strong though life bends and twists
So far from love was I ever in reach? I cast a vote
Through it all, I'm going strong though its murder love wrote
Days turn to years as I wonder will it end
Through it all, I'm going strong though I've lost loves trend
Nights turn to tears, and with the darkness, it blends
Though it all I'm going strong though I wish to ascend
Whose love am I after? Which one should I choose?
Through it all, I'm going strong though love seems to refuse
Too many women on my conscience keep me quite amused
through it all I'm going strong though my heart they use

Kush Ha Mim

Way back when

I remember way back when we used to ...
Um ... When we used to be in love
Way back then, we were so ...
Um ... Way back then, we were so in love
Way back when we used to ...
Um ... Way back when we used to make love
I remember way back then the things we used to ...
Um ... The things we used to do out of love
Way back then, you were young and ...
Um ... Way back then, you were young and in love
I remember way back when I drove you ...
Um ... Way back when I drove you crazy in love
Way back then we to ... Um ... Cherish our love
I remember way back when I told you ... Um ...
Um ... That I was in love
Way back then, you told me ... Um ... Back then, you told me we'll always be in love
Way back when I used to ...
Um ... Back when I used to blow your mind with love
Do you remember way back then?
Um ... Way back when ... Um ... Um ... Way back when we used to ... Um ...
Way back when we used to ... When we used to ...

Um ... When we used to ... Um ... When we used to be in love?
Um ... Do you?

Kush Ha Mim

When I was where I was

What's done is done; that's how I feel
What's to come will come its how we deal
What's gone is gone can't receive that back
Call a pawn a pawn can't deceive that fact
What do you think? Just let me know
Watch us sink; they would love that show
But we'll strive for better or worse
Come alive, come alive Love is the purse
I need you; I need you, But what am I to do
I bleed you Just watching you two
When I was where I was, I was far much better
Now love does what it does a storm I must weather
Curious, curious, and now I see
Furious, furious No room for three

Kush Ha Mim

Heartfelt

Without you, I'm living a lie living to die
A void of incompletion encompasses my soul
You've been gone for too long your presence oblige
Loneliness seems to engulf me whole
Without you, there's no us without us; there's no comfort
Greatness and glory cannot sublimate grief a broker
is yet to be found that can value your worth you're a precious thought invading my fief
Without you, I suffocate in my mind's dilemma
Trap in a purgatory trance Confused in a maze of a mysterious enigma
A war with my conscience fought with a lance
Without you, as my bride, my world divides; my thoughts are inspired by mirrors of the past; my heart's a castle where no one resides
What's paradise if you've gotten there without a task?
Without you, no pain can describe No heart can endure half my duress
My thoughts bleed along with the words that I scribe
I live for the moment without you more or less

Kush Ha Mim

I'm just saying

I am doing the best that I can
Nothing is going according to my plan
I didn't consult with the most high
And the beginning to my end draws nigh
I do wish for a future loving you
As I cry your name, the angels say, who?
Our love has been long forgotten
Left on the side of love's highway to rotten
My emotions come, my emotions go
Someone else will reap what I left to sew
I must consult with the All Compassionate
When love comes back around, I shall cast a net
I must clear my thoughts to clear my mind
I'm wrapped in lost love, and you're my bind
But I won't give up on you believe in me
My greatest failure is you leaving me

Kush Ha Mim

The shape of my heart

Times are going, but my love is still yours
My heart is showing like a beacon from the shores
Somewhere out there, I hope someone care
I hope I'm not forgotten with the heavy heart I bare
Young and lonely those I love are at a distance
And oh, if only! They could be here this instance
To help me cope with it all, a heart in exile
To help me if I fall warm hugs and smiles
The shape of my heart molded so skillfully; what shape is it now?
Love molds so willfully, But I'm still yours all whom love is still mine
I'm drifting in the balance though all is still fine
Longing for a new day, the love is stale in health
The shape of my heart changes so love so frail in wealth
Times are going, and I'm going with my heart's emotion
For somewhere out there is my love to cleanse the corrosion

Kush Ha Mim

Exiled Outside Looking In

At the breaking point, I breakdown cause and effect
I've found a breakthrough I'm not looking out but in
And while soaring in love, my heart must pause and direct
Love is a treacherous game with no rules; just win
They say no love reaches the outskirts, is that so?
Apparently, I'm misinformed, but I've been hanging on
An outsider locked out from love as it glows
In the battle with love, I stumble though I've been lagging on
Hearts cry out with mine singing of love off-key
I turn to better times; it's all an optical illusion
Where does it end or begin? Or all the jokes off me?
Who's laughing? This is all love's typical confusion
I'm elated in my dreaming state I shun reality
And get a rare glimpse of love from my outpost position
Out casted I'm deprived of love's confidentiality
I lead a one-man army love has no opposition
Yet stubborn, I battle love through my dexterity
Exiled, I drown in pools of tears I didn't cry
Outside it's a mirage I bask in austerity
Exiled I'm paying for a life's worth I didn't buy

Kush Ha Mim

Robert N. Nicholas Jr, aka Kush Abdul mutakabbir Ha Mim who is most commonly known as Kush Ha Mim.

Peace and blessings to you all, and welcome to the mind of a distraught Jamaican Muslim immigrant poet as I scribe about lost love and all that comes with it being in exile; my pen bleeds my pain as I wait for the moment that I've been waiting on peace and blessings.

www.ingramcontent.com/pod-product-compliance
Lightning Source LLC
La Vergne TN
LVHW092008090526
838202LV00001B/49

9781957208329